CRIMCOMICS

ANOMIE AND STRAIN THEORIES

KRISTA S. GEHRING

WRITER

MICHAEL R. BATISTA

ARTIST

CHERYL L. WALLACE

LETTERER

D1413581

New York   Oxford

OXFORD UNIVERSITY PRESS

FOREWORD

Criminologists develop theories of crime with the hope that such theories will help to reduce crime. If we want to stop individuals from offending, we must know what causes them to engage in crime. We can then make an effort to address those causes. But crime theories will have little effect unless they are widely disseminated, both to policy makers and to the general public. If people believe that offenders engage in crime simply because they are bad or evil people (e.g., "superpredators"), they will not support programs designed to address the true causes of crime. But if people believe that crime results from issues such as strains or stressors, they may try to alleviate the causes.

Unfortunately, criminologists have not had much success in disseminating their work to wider audiences. I believe that the *CrimComics* series is a great way to let people know about the core ideas of leading crime theories. Many people don't like reading textbooks or academic articles, but comic books have a reputation for being both accessible and exciting. *CrimComics* build on this reputation by telling the engaging stories behind the development of leading crime theories. In doing so, they illustrate the core ideas of these theories.

To be sure, *CrimComics* do not focus on superheroes battling for their lives or trying to save the planet from annihilation. But like traditional comic books, *CrimComics* focus on individuals involved in a struggle to make the world a better place. The struggle is intellectual, with criminologists trying to determine why individuals engage in crime, responding to criticisms that others might make of their theory, and revising the theories when necessary.

Take my own general strain theory, one of the theories presented in this issue. Based on my life experience and studies, I had a strong suspicion that many individuals engage in crime to cope with the strains or stressors they encounter. For example, people engage in theft to cope with financial problems. But I struggled for a long time to describe the particular strains most likely to cause crime. Some strains, such as financial problems and parental rejection, are conducive to crime, while others, such as the burdens associated with caring for family members, may not be.

Also, I struggled to explain why some people are more likely than others to cope with the strains they experience through crime. Most people cope with their problems through legal means. For example, they deal with financial problems by getting a second job or cutting back on expenses. Only a small percentage cope through crime, but it is critical to describe the factors that promote criminal coping. Further, I struggled to respond to certain criticisms of the theory. For example, how does the theory explain crime among groups that appear to be low in strain, such as middle- and upper-class individuals? And how does the theory explain why males are more criminal than females, although females experience as much or more strain than males?

The feature I most like about *CrimComics* is that they describe these struggles and, more generally, the factors that influenced criminologists as they developed their theories. Unlike many texts, they do not present crime theories as if they emerged out of thin air and are engraved in stone. Rather, they describe the origin of these theories and how they changed over time. For example, I grew up in a community with a high level of crime. My observations and experience suggested that many juveniles who engaged in crime did so in response to strains such

as physical and verbal abuse, experiences with discrimination, and family problems. This is not to say that the type of strain emphasized by Merton—the inability to achieve the cultural goal of economic success through legitimate means—is unimportant. Rather, other types of strain also contribute to crime. Why Merton came to focus on the blockage of economic goals is understandable. As this issue points out, Merton's theory was developed during the major economic crisis in our country's history, the Depression. And this type of strain is one of the key strains in general strain theory. General strain theory builds on Merton's theory, but also extends the theory, drawing on my own experience and recent research in several areas.

I hope that you enjoy *CrimComics* as I have, and I invite you to read them with a critical eye. Do the theories presented make sense to you? Do they jibe with your experiences and what you have learned in other courses? How might you build on or revise these theories? Also, ask yourself how these theories might be applied to reduce crime in the larger community.

ROBERT AGNEW
Emory University

PREFACE

In the United States, there is a societal belief that if you work hard enough, *anyone* can achieve the "American Dream." The concept of the American Dream is socialized deep in the consciousness of U.S. citizens from a very young age—people are indoctrinated to believe that they must pursue material success through open, individual competition in a capitalist society. This belief is also known in other countries—many, many individuals come to America with the belief that they too will be able to have a piece of the proverbial pie. This is the land of opportunity and they will be able to make a better life for themselves and their families here.

The idea of the American Dream appears to be relatively positive—work hard and you will be rewarded. However, in 1938, Robert Merton proposed that the notion was instead criminogenic and could explain the high crime rates in America. Striving for a goal such as the American Dream is a positive activity, but if access to legitimate and legal means to reach the goal is not equal for everyone, some people may use illegitimate means (including criminal activity) to achieve it. Because the culture structure and the class structure are not integrated, anomie occurs and frees people to pursue the goal through any means possible. This idea is timeless; even today there are individuals who work hard but still are unable to even make ends meet. If they want the American Dream, how can they achieve it?

Indeed, America places a great emphasis on the economy and acquiring money. This is illustrated further by Messner and Rosenfeld's extension of Merton's theory and their focus on how social institutions (i.e., family, religion, education) were subservient to the economy. For example, education is seen as a means to achieve employment. When I ask my students why they are in college, the automatic reply is "To get a better job." This played out in my own life when I was attending college. When I was an undergraduate student, I went through a series of changes to my major. First, I was an anthropology major—I wanted to dig up bones and artifacts and be an archeologist. After taking a few courses and coming to believe that I would not be able to make any money that way, I changed my major to kinesiology. I thought I could be a physical therapist and make a lot of money. But after having trouble with the required biology classes (and knowing I had to take additional classes in the sciences, which I was not strong in), I had a meltdown in the kitchen of the house I shared with four friends. I kept telling my roommate I couldn't do this and I needed to change my major. The strain was too great, and I did not believe it was a good idea to pursue that major just because I thought I could make a lot of money. I remember her telling me that I should wait one more semester to see how it went, but I knew that if I didn't do well in biology, I wasn't going to do well in chemistry and all the other courses I had to take. I left, went to campus, and changed my major to English.

When I sat in my first English course, I knew I had made the right decision. I felt like I had finally found something that I not only enjoyed, but also was good at. However, whenever someone asked me what my major was, I was inevitably met with the response "What are you going to do with that?" I wasn't ridiculed, but I could tell that my academic pursuits were not taken as seriously as those of students who were pursuing majors that would guarantee better employment prospects. Little did I know that many years later I would be in a career that required a significant amount of writing and that my degree would also come in handy writing comic books. Now I'm living *my* American Dream with a career that doesn't feel like work because I enjoy it so much.

As with any book project, *CrimComics* consumed much time and effort, perhaps more so than a traditional textbook. Thinking about theory—and, in particular, trying to design a work that best conveys the theories in a visual medium—is fun. Still, with busy lives, finding the space in the day to carefully research, write, illustrate, ink,

and letter the pages of this work is a source of some stress. We were fortunate to have had an amazing amount of support during these times from family, friends, and Oxford University Press. We also want to acknowledge the talents of Cheryl Wallace. Cheryl's flair for lettering allowed us to get our ideas across to the readers.

The support of these and so many other individuals has made the creation of *CrimComics* possible and a rewarding experience for us. We would like to thank the following reviewers: Viviana Andreescu, University of Louisville; Ellen G. Cohn, Florida International University; Tammy S. Garland, University of Tennessee Chattanooga; J. Mitchell Miller, University of North Florida; Elizabeth Perkins, Morehead State University; Harold A. Wells, Tennessee State University. We hope that this and other issues of *CrimComics* will inspire passion in your students to learn criminological theory.

Anomie and Strain Theories

SOUTH PHILADELPHIA, 1925.

MEYER ROBERT SCHKOLNICK WAS THE SON OF WORKING-CLASS EASTERN EUROPEAN JEWISH IMMIGRANTS.

HE GREW UP IN THE SLUMS OF SOUTH PHILADELPHIA.

HEY CHARLES! WHERE'VE YOU BEEN? MY SISTER HAS BEEN WAITING FOR YOU.

HEY MEYER. I GOT CAUGHT TALKING TO THAT SHOE MAKER ON THE CORNER AGAIN. HE WAS TALKING ABOUT KARL MARX AGAIN.

OH YEAH—HE'S BEEN TALKING TO ME ABOUT MARX SINCE I WAS FIVE OR SIX. I JUST READ DAS CAPITAL AND IT WAS PRETTY INTERESTING.

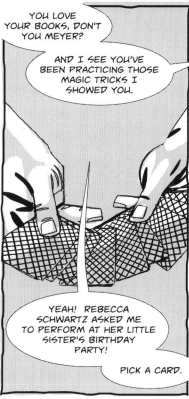

YOU LOVE YOUR BOOKS, DON'T YOU MEYER?

AND I SEE YOU'VE BEEN PRACTICING THOSE MAGIC TRICKS I SHOWED YOU.

YEAH! REBECCA SCHWARTZ ASKED ME TO PERFORM AT HER LITTLE SISTER'S BIRTHDAY PARTY!

PICK A CARD.

WHAT ARE YOU GOING TO CALL YOUR ACT? "MEYER THE MAGICIAN"?

"THE MAGNIFICENT MEYER"?

NO—I NEED SOMETHING WITH A BIT MORE PIZZAZZ, DON'T YOU THINK?

ACTORS AND ACTRESSES ADOPT STAGE NAMES ALL THE TIME--I THINK I WILL TOO!

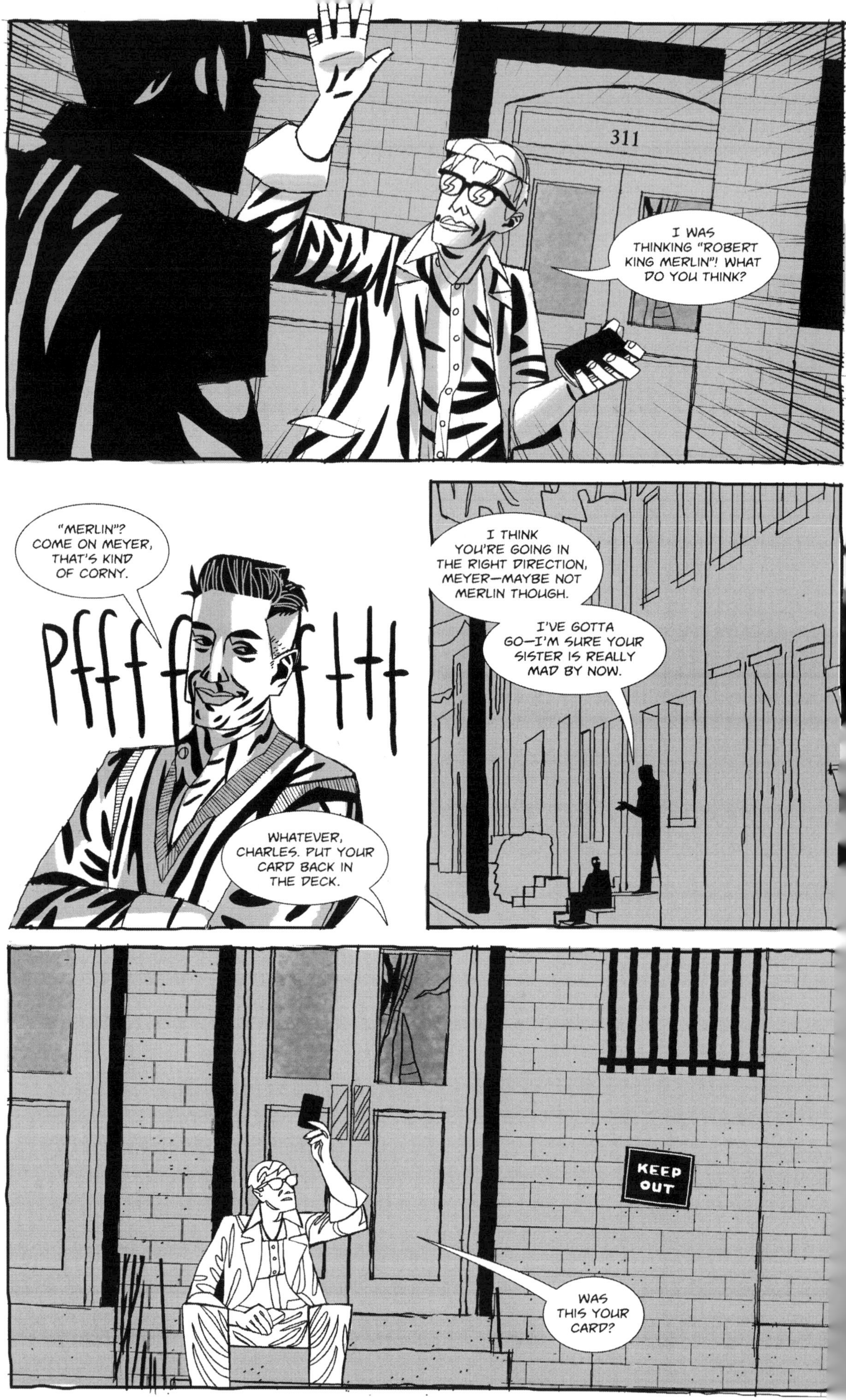
311
I WAS THINKING "ROBERT KING MERLIN"! WHAT DO YOU THINK?
"MERLIN"? COME ON MEYER, THAT'S KIND OF CORNY.
PFFFFFTTT
WHATEVER, CHARLES. PUT YOUR CARD BACK IN THE DECK.
I THINK YOU'RE GOING IN THE RIGHT DIRECTION, MEYER—MAYBE NOT MERLIN THOUGH.
I'VE GOTTA GO—I'M SURE YOUR SISTER IS REALLY MAD BY NOW.
KEEP OUT
WAS THIS YOUR CARD?

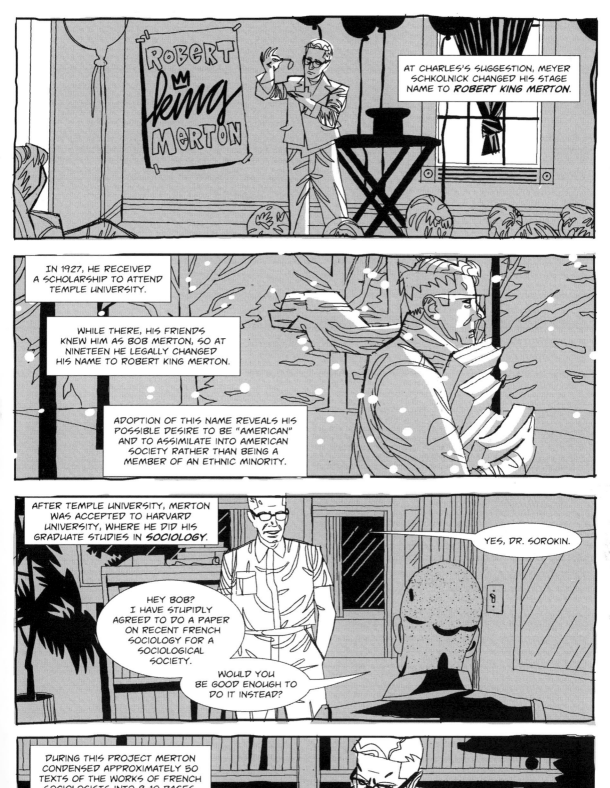

AT CHARLES'S SUGGESTION, MEYER SCHKOLNICK CHANGED HIS STAGE NAME TO *ROBERT KING MERTON.*

IN 1927, HE RECEIVED A SCHOLARSHIP TO ATTEND TEMPLE UNIVERSITY.

WHILE THERE, HIS FRIENDS KNEW HIM AS BOB MERTON, SO AT NINETEEN HE LEGALLY CHANGED HIS NAME TO ROBERT KING MERTON.

ADOPTION OF THIS NAME REVEALS HIS POSSIBLE DESIRE TO BE "AMERICAN" AND TO ASSIMILATE INTO AMERICAN SOCIETY RATHER THAN BEING A MEMBER OF AN ETHNIC MINORITY.

AFTER TEMPLE UNIVERSITY, MERTON WAS ACCEPTED TO HARVARD UNIVERSITY, WHERE HE DID HIS GRADUATE STUDIES IN *SOCIOLOGY.*

YES, DR. SOROKIN.

HEY BOB? I HAVE STUPIDLY AGREED TO DO A PAPER ON RECENT FRENCH SOCIOLOGY FOR A SOCIOLOGICAL SOCIETY.

WOULD YOU BE GOOD ENOUGH TO DO IT INSTEAD?

DURING THIS PROJECT MERTON CONDENSED APPROXIMATELY 50 TEXTS OF THE WORKS OF FRENCH SOCIOLOGISTS INTO 8-10 PAGES.

MERTON FOUND THE WRITINGS OF *EMILE DURKHEIM* TO BE PARTICULARLY INTRIGUING...

SUICIDE

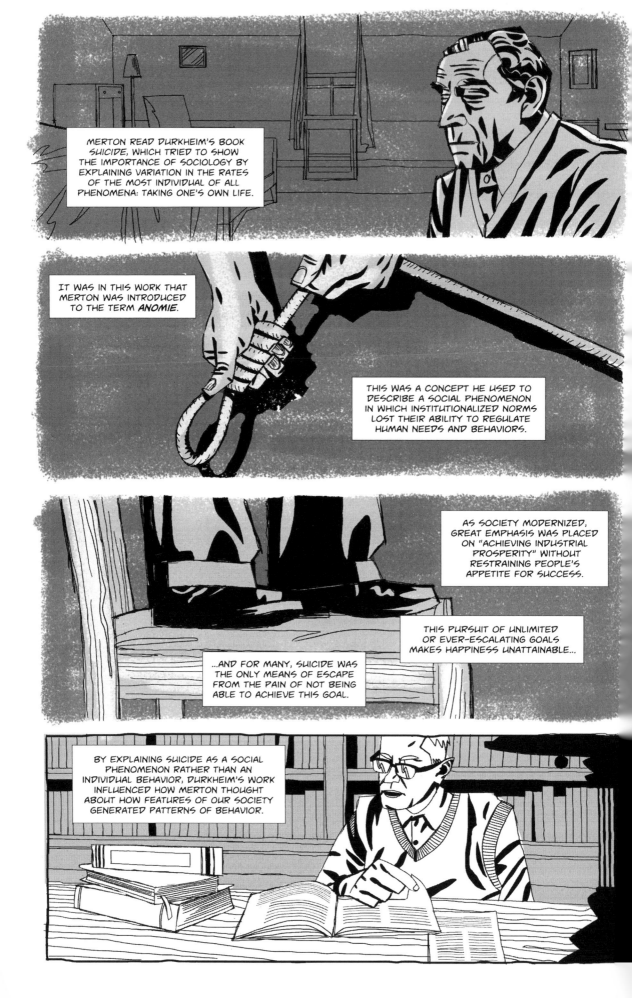

MERTON READ DURKHEIM'S BOOK *SUICIDE*, WHICH TRIED TO SHOW THE IMPORTANCE OF SOCIOLOGY BY EXPLAINING VARIATION IN THE RATES OF THE MOST INDIVIDUAL OF ALL PHENOMENA: TAKING ONE'S OWN LIFE.

IT WAS IN THIS WORK THAT MERTON WAS INTRODUCED TO THE TERM *ANOMIE*.

THIS WAS A CONCEPT HE USED TO DESCRIBE A SOCIAL PHENOMENON IN WHICH INSTITUTIONALIZED NORMS LOST THEIR ABILITY TO REGULATE HUMAN NEEDS AND BEHAVIORS.

AS SOCIETY MODERNIZED, GREAT EMPHASIS WAS PLACED ON "ACHIEVING INDUSTRIAL PROSPERITY" WITHOUT RESTRAINING PEOPLE'S APPETITE FOR SUCCESS.

THIS PURSUIT OF UNLIMITED OR EVER-ESCALATING GOALS MAKES HAPPINESS UNATTAINABLE...

...AND FOR MANY, SUICIDE WAS THE ONLY MEANS OF ESCAPE FROM THE PAIN OF NOT BEING ABLE TO ACHIEVE THIS GOAL.

BY EXPLAINING SUICIDE AS A SOCIAL PHENOMENON RATHER THAN AN INDIVIDUAL BEHAVIOR, DURKHEIM'S WORK INFLUENCED HOW MERTON THOUGHT ABOUT HOW FEATURES OF OUR SOCIETY GENERATED PATTERNS OF BEHAVIOR.

WHILE MERTON PURSUED HIS STUDIES, SOME KEY EVENTS HAPPENED IN THE UNITED STATES THAT LIKELY ALSO INFLUENCED HOW HE THOUGHT ABOUT HUMAN BEHAVIOR.

FOR EXAMPLE, PROHIBITION BEGAN IN 1920 WITH THE PASSAGE OF THE EIGHTEENTH AMENDMENT THAT BANNED THE PRODUCTION, IMPORTATION, TRANSPORTATION, AND SALE OF ALCOHOLIC BEVERAGES.

BOOTLEGGING AND OTHER CRIMES INCREASED, WITH MANY INDIVIDUALS BECOMING WEALTHY AND POWERFUL WITHIN ORGANIZED CRIME SYNDICATES.

ON OCTOBER 29, 1929, THE STOCK MARKET CRASHED. BILLIONS OF DOLLARS WERE LOST, WIPING OUT THOUSANDS OF INVESTORS.

BLACK TUESDAY

STOCK MARKET CRASH

THIS CAUSED AMERICA AND THE REST OF THE INDUSTRIALIZED WORLD TO SPIRAL DOWNWARD INTO THE *GREAT DEPRESSION* (1929–39).

THIS WAS THE DEEPEST AND LONGEST-LASTING ECONOMIC DOWNTURN IN THE HISTORY OF THE WESTERN INDUSTRIALIZED WORLD UP TO THAT TIME.

FREE COFFEE & DONUTS FOR THE UN-EMPLOYED

BY 1933, NEARLY HALF OF AMERICA'S BANKS HAD FAILED, AND UNEMPLOYMENT WAS APPROACHING 15 MILLION PEOPLE, OR 30 PERCENT OF THE WORKFORCE.

AND DURING THIS TIME, MANY SCHOLARS ADVOCATED FOR BIOLOGICAL EXPLANATIONS OF CRIMINAL BEHAVIOR, MANY OF WHICH FOCUSED ON CRIMINAL ANTHROPOLOGY, FEEBLE-MINDEDNESS, AND INFERIOR PHYSICAL CONSTITUTIONS.*

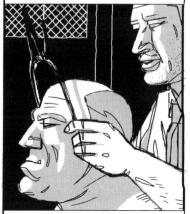

*FOR MORE INFORMATION, CHECK OUT CRIMCOMICS: BIOLOGY AND CRIMINALITY!

IN 1935, MERTON RECEIVED HIS DOCTORATE FROM HARVARD AND BECAME A FACULTY MEMBER THERE.

WHILE THERE, HIS INFLUENTIAL ARTICLE "SOCIAL STRUCTURE AND ANOMIE" (1938) WAS PUBLISHED.

AT A TIME WHEN THEORIZING ABOUT CRIMINALS FOCUSED ON INDIVIDUAL TRAITS, MERTON DEVELOPED A THEORY THAT FOCUSED ON DEVELOPING A SOCIOLOGICAL EXPLANATION FOR CRIME IN AMERICA.

Social Structure and Anomie

Social Structure and Anomie

AH, YOU HAVE ACTUALLY PREPARED FOR CLASS TODAY, MR. PERKINS!

I AM VERY FAMILIAR WITH THE WRITINGS OF THE CHICAGO CRIMINOLOGISTS.

PROFESSOR MERTON, WHY DOESN'T YOUR ARTICLE FOCUS ON THE NEIGHBORHOOD AFFECTING CRIME? ISN'T THAT WHAT IS COMING OUT OF THE UNIVERSITY OF CHICAGO RIGHT NOW?

WHILE THEY FOCUS ON STRUCTURAL VARIABLES UNIQUE TO THE INNER-CITY SLUMS,* I PROPOSE THAT AMERICAN SOCIETY IN GENERAL IS AT THE CORE OF THE NATION'S CRIME AND DEVIANCE.

*CHECK OUT CRIMCOMICS: SOCIAL DISORGANIZATION THEORY FOR MORE INFORMATION!

I GREW UP IN THE SLUMS OF PHILADELPHIA. MY FAMILY WAS POOR AND LIVED IN A DEPRESSED AREA.

I REMEMBER NEIGHBORHOOD GANGS AND CRIME HAPPENING THERE—BUT MY LIFE IN THE SLUMS WAS NOT RIDDLED WITH CULTURE CONFLICT AS THE CHICAGO SOCIOLOGISTS PROPOSE.

"I WAS PROVIDED EVERY SORT OF CAPITAL—SOCIAL CAPITAL, CULTURAL CAPITAL, HUMAN CAPITAL, AND, ABOVE ALL, WHAT WE MAY CALL PUBLIC CAPITAL—THAT IS, WITH EVERY SORT OF CAPITAL EXCEPT THE PERSONALLY FINANCIAL."

"I WAS AFFORDED MANY OPPORTUNITIES."

"FOR EXAMPLE, EVEN THOUGH I LIVED IN THE SLUMS, I OFTEN ACCESSED PUBLIC VENUES THAT WERE EDUCATIONALLY AND CULTURALLY ENRICHING."

"I VIEW WHERE I LIVED AS A SORT OF 'BENIGN SLUM.'"

"DURING THIS TIME, THERE WAS A SENSE THAT WE ALL HAD LIMITLESS POSSIBILITIES, EVEN THOUGH MANY OF US WERE FROM IMPOVERISHED CIRCUMSTANCES."

"ANYONE COULD SEEK SOCIAL MOBILITY AND EXPECT TO ENJOY A MEASURE OF SUCCESS."

"BUT THIS IDEA CAN BE PROBLEMATIC FOR SOME..."

IN 1939, MERTON LEFT HARVARD AND BECAME A PROFESSOR AND CHAIRMAN OF THE SOCIOLOGY DEPARTMENT AT TULANE UNIVERSITY.

SOCIETY CONSISTS OF A *CULTURAL STRUCTURE* AND A *SOCIAL STRUCTURE.*

THE *CULTURAL* STRUCTURE HAS TWO COMPONENTS. THE FIRST CONSISTS OF CULTURALLY DEFINED GOALS, PURPOSES, AND INTERESTS.

"THE 'AMERICAN DREAM' IS A UNIVERSAL CULTURALLY DEFINED GOAL THAT ALL CITIZENS OF THE UNITED STATES ARE ENCOURAGED TO STRIVE FOR. AMERICA PLACES GREAT IMPORTANCE ON ECONOMIC AFFLUENCE AND SOCIAL ASCENT FOR ALL ITS MEMBERS. THAT IS, FINANCIAL SUCCESS IS A CORE GOAL OF AMERICAN SOCIETY. THE SECOND COMPONENT OF THE CULTURAL STRUCTURE IS *INSTITUTIONAL NORMS,* THAT IS, ACCEPTABLE MODES OF ACHIEVING THESE GOALS, LIKE WORKING HARD AT A LEGITIMATE JOB."

IN OTHER WORDS, WE TELL EVERYONE THAT THEY MUST STRIVE FOR THE GOALS OF FINANCIAL SUCCESS--THE "AMERICAN DREAM"--BUT NOT EVERYONE HAS EQUAL OPPORTUNITIES TO ACHIEVE THOSE GOALS.

BECAUSE OF THIS, INDIVIDUALS WHO DON'T HAVE ACCESS TO LEGITIMATE MEANS TO REACH THE AMERICAN DREAM WILL SEEK OUT ILLEGITIMATE WAYS TO REACH THAT GOAL.

IN THE UNITED STATES, ONE OF THESE GOALS IS THE *AMERICAN DREAM*.*

THAT IS, "THAT DREAM OF A LAND IN WHICH LIFE SHOULD BE BETTER AND RICHER AND FULLER FOR EVERY MAN, WITH OPPORTUNITY FOR EACH ACCORDING TO HIS ABILITY OR ACHIEVEMENT... REGARDLESS OF THE FORTUITOUS CIRCUMSTANCES OF BIRTH OR POSITION."

"THE SOCIAL STRUCTURE RELATES TO CLASS STRATIFICATION. FOR SOME, THE SOCIAL STRUCTURE LIMITS ACCESS TO THE GOAL OF SUCCESS THROUGH LEGITIMATE MEANS. FOR THOSE OF YOU WHO HAVE READ KARL MARX AND HIS IDEAS ABOUT CLASS STRUGGLE, THIS MAY SOUND FAMILIAR. WHEN PEOPLE DO NOT HAVE THE INSTITUTIONAL MEANS TO REACH CULTURALLY PRESCRIBED GOALS, IT CAUSES STRAIN ON THE INSTITUTIONAL NORMS. THE NORMS THEN LOSE THEIR LEGITIMACY AND REGULATORY POWER. WHEN THE NORMS WEAKEN AND CAN NO LONGER REGULATE PEOPLE, 'ANOMIE' OCCURS. PEOPLE ARE THEN FREE TO 'INNOVATE' AND USE THE MOST SELF-SERVING MEANS, INCLUDING CRIME, TO PURSUE GOALS."

THEREFORE, THE MUCH-VALUED IDEA OF THE AMERICAN DREAM IS IMPLICATED IN AN UNANTICIPATED WAY IN THE SOCIAL PRODUCTION OF CRIME AND DEVIANCE IN AMERICA.

*THE TERM AMERICAN DREAM WAS COINED BY JAMES TRUSLOW ADAMS IN HIS BOOK *THE EPIC OF AMERICA* (1931).

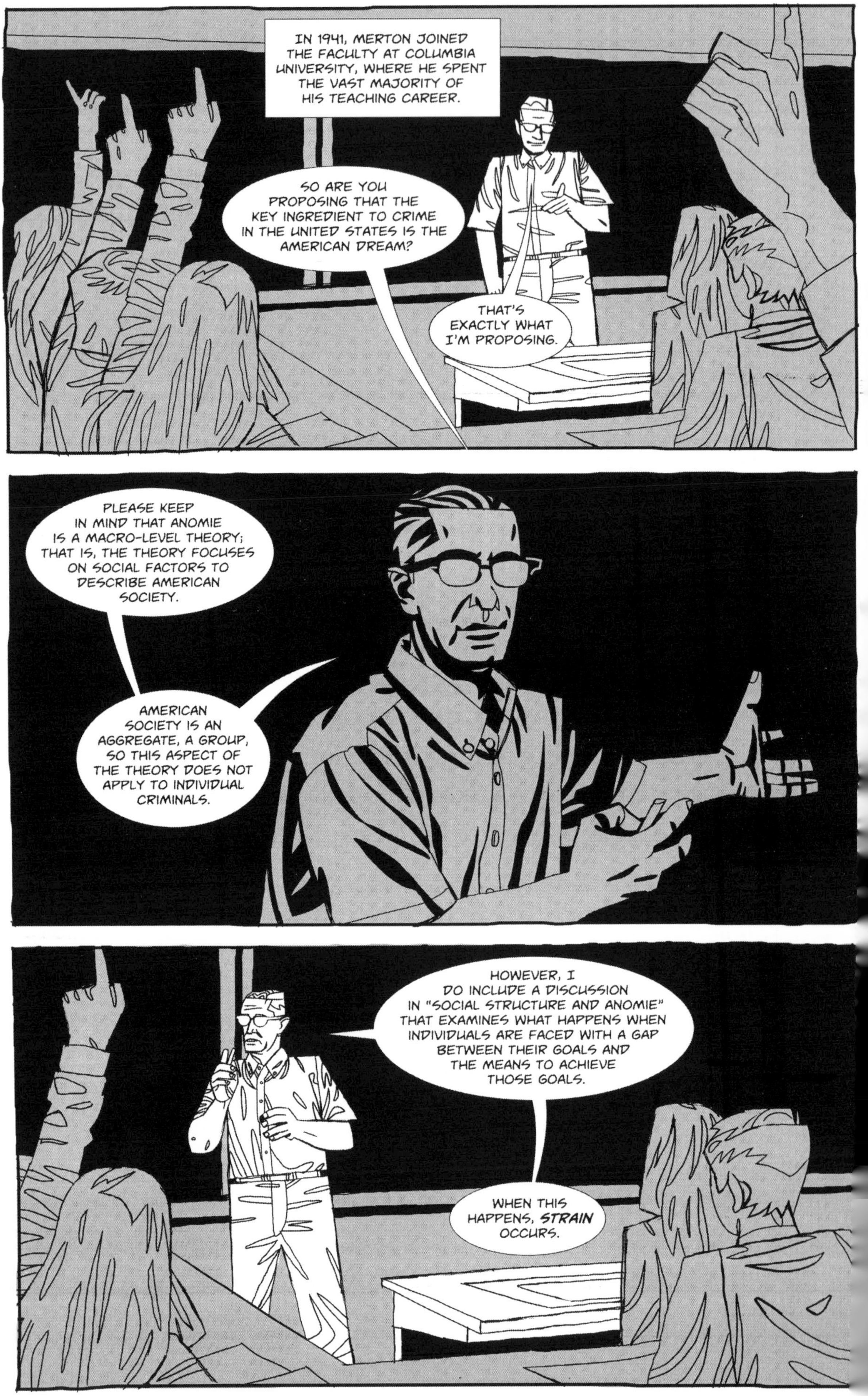

IN 1941, MERTON JOINED THE FACULTY AT COLUMBIA UNIVERSITY, WHERE HE SPENT THE VAST MAJORITY OF HIS TEACHING CAREER.
SO ARE YOU PROPOSING THAT THE KEY INGREDIENT TO CRIME IN THE UNITED STATES IS THE AMERICAN DREAM?
THAT'S EXACTLY WHAT I'M PROPOSING.
PLEASE KEEP IN MIND THAT ANOMIE IS A MACRO-LEVEL THEORY; THAT IS, THE THEORY FOCUSES ON SOCIAL FACTORS TO DESCRIBE AMERICAN SOCIETY.
AMERICAN SOCIETY IS AN AGGREGATE, A GROUP, SO THIS ASPECT OF THE THEORY DOES NOT APPLY TO INDIVIDUAL CRIMINALS.
HOWEVER, I DO INCLUDE A DISCUSSION IN "SOCIAL STRUCTURE AND ANOMIE" THAT EXAMINES WHAT HAPPENS WHEN INDIVIDUALS ARE FACED WITH A GAP BETWEEN THEIR GOALS AND THE MEANS TO ACHIEVE THOSE GOALS.
WHEN THIS HAPPENS, **STRAIN** OCCURS.

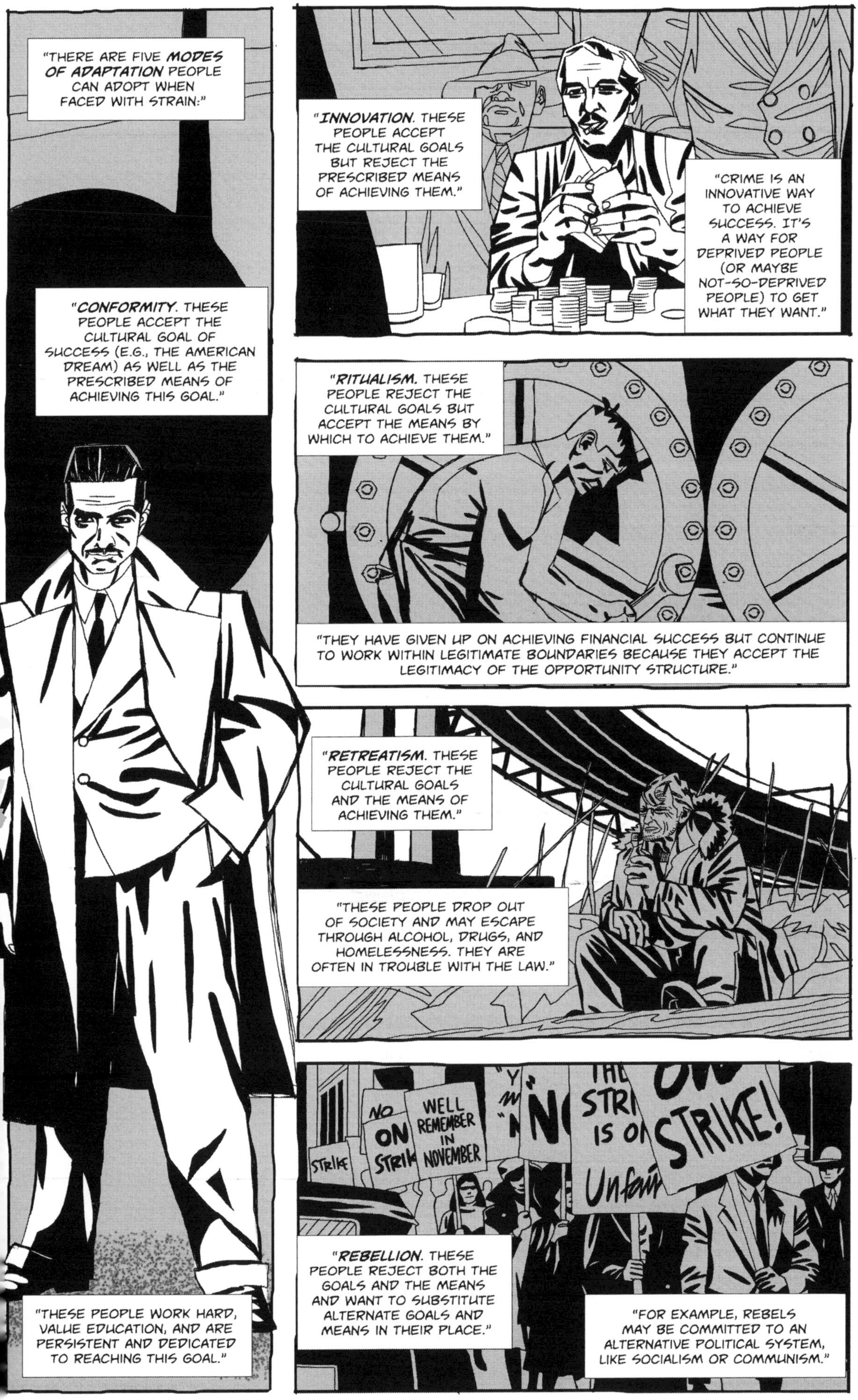
"THERE ARE FIVE ***MODES OF ADAPTATION*** PEOPLE CAN ADOPT WHEN FACED WITH STRAIN:"
"***CONFORMITY***. THESE PEOPLE ACCEPT THE CULTURAL GOAL OF SUCCESS (E.G., THE AMERICAN DREAM) AS WELL AS THE PRESCRIBED MEANS OF ACHIEVING THIS GOAL."
"THESE PEOPLE WORK HARD, VALUE EDUCATION, AND ARE PERSISTENT AND DEDICATED TO REACHING THIS GOAL."
"***INNOVATION***. THESE PEOPLE ACCEPT THE CULTURAL GOALS BUT REJECT THE PRESCRIBED MEANS OF ACHIEVING THEM."
"CRIME IS AN INNOVATIVE WAY TO ACHIEVE SUCCESS. IT'S A WAY FOR DEPRIVED PEOPLE (OR MAYBE NOT-SO-DEPRIVED PEOPLE) TO GET WHAT THEY WANT."
"***RITUALISM.*** THESE PEOPLE REJECT THE CULTURAL GOALS BUT ACCEPT THE MEANS BY WHICH TO ACHIEVE THEM."
"THEY HAVE GIVEN UP ON ACHIEVING FINANCIAL SUCCESS BUT CONTINUE TO WORK WITHIN LEGITIMATE BOUNDARIES BECAUSE THEY ACCEPT THE LEGITIMACY OF THE OPPORTUNITY STRUCTURE."
"***RETREATISM***. THESE PEOPLE REJECT THE CULTURAL GOALS AND THE MEANS OF ACHIEVING THEM."
"THESE PEOPLE DROP OUT OF SOCIETY AND MAY ESCAPE THROUGH ALCOHOL, DRUGS, AND HOMELESSNESS. THEY ARE OFTEN IN TROUBLE WITH THE LAW."
WELL REMEMBER IN NOVEMBER
STRIKE
STRIKE!
"***REBELLION***. THESE PEOPLE REJECT BOTH THE GOALS AND THE MEANS AND WANT TO SUBSTITUTE ALTERNATE GOALS AND MEANS IN THEIR PLACE."
"FOR EXAMPLE, REBELS MAY BE COMMITTED TO AN ALTERNATIVE POLITICAL SYSTEM, LIKE SOCIALISM OR COMMUNISM."

MERTON'S LIFE SEEMS TO MIRROR THE "AMERICAN DREAM."

311

BORN IN THE SLUMS OF SOUTH PHILADELPHIA...

...HE ASCENDED TO A PROFESSORSHIP AT COLUMBIA UNIVERSITY AND ULTIMATELY BECAME PERHAPS THE MOST FAMOUS SOCIOLOGIST OF THE 20TH CENTURY.

HOWEVER, "SOCIAL STRUCTURE AND ANOMIE" DID NOT RECEIVE WIDE-SPREAD ATTENTION UNTIL TWO DECADES LATER WHEN MERTON'S FORMER STUDENTS USED HIS IDEAS TO DEVELOP WHAT ARE KNOWN AS SUBCULTURAL THEORIES.*

ALSO, IN THE 1960S, A SHIFT IN THINKING LED MANY TO VIEW ISSUES OF CRIME AND POVERTY AS MAJOR SOCIAL PROBLEMS, NOT THE FAULT OF THE INDIVIDUAL.

BECAUSE OF THIS, A "WAR ON POVERTY" WAS INITIATED BY PRESIDENT LYNDON B. JOHNSON THAT LED TO MANY OF THE FEDERAL AND STATE INITIATIVES LOW-INCOME AMERICANS RELY ON TODAY.

IDEAS CAUSE REACTIONS.

FURTHERMORE, THE CIVIL RIGHTS MOVEMENT BROUGHT ATTENTION TO THE ISSUE OF MINORITIES AND DISADVANTAGED CITIZENS BEING DENIED OPPORTUNITIES.

*FIND OUT MORE ABOUT THIS IN CRIMCOMICS: SUBCULTURAL THEORIES!

ATLANTIC CITY, 1965.

AS A BOY GROWING UP DURING THE 1950S AND 1960S IN ATLANTIC CITY'S IMPOVERISHED "INLET" NEIGHBORHOOD, *ROBERT AGNEW* WAS INTENSELY AWARE OF HOW SOCIAL FACTORS SHAPED ONE'S EXPERIENCES.

THE NEIGHBORHOOD HE LIVED IN HAD SHARP SOCIAL DIVISIONS— THE VARIOUS RACIAL AND ETHNIC GROUPS THAT RESIDED THERE DID NOT INTERACT WITH EACH OTHER.

IT WAS DIFFICULT TO LIVE IN THIS SORT OF A SOCIAL ENVIRONMENT, BUT IT ULTIMATELY SHAPED HOW HE THOUGHT ABOUT BEHAVIOR.

IN HIGH SCHOOL, HE WROTE HIS FIRST "SOCIOLOGICAL" PAPER THAT DISCUSSED THE WAYS RACE/ETHNICITY AND CLASS AFFECTED ACADEMIC ACHIEVEMENT.*

SOCIAL LOCATION HAS AN ENORMOUS EFFECT ON A PERSON'S EXPERIENCES, BELIEFS, AND BEHAVIOR.

RUTGERS UNIVERSITY, 1972.

BY THE TIME AGNEW LEFT FOR COLLEGE, HE HAD A STRONG INTEREST IN HOW THE SOCIAL ENVIRONMENT INFLUENCED INDIVIDUALS, PARTICULARLY IN NEGATIVE WAYS.

IT WAS HERE HE TOOK AN INTRODUCTORY SOCIOLOGY COURSE AND FELL IN LOVE WITH THE DISCIPLINE.

*A TOPIC KEY TO THE THEORY HE LATER DEVELOPED...

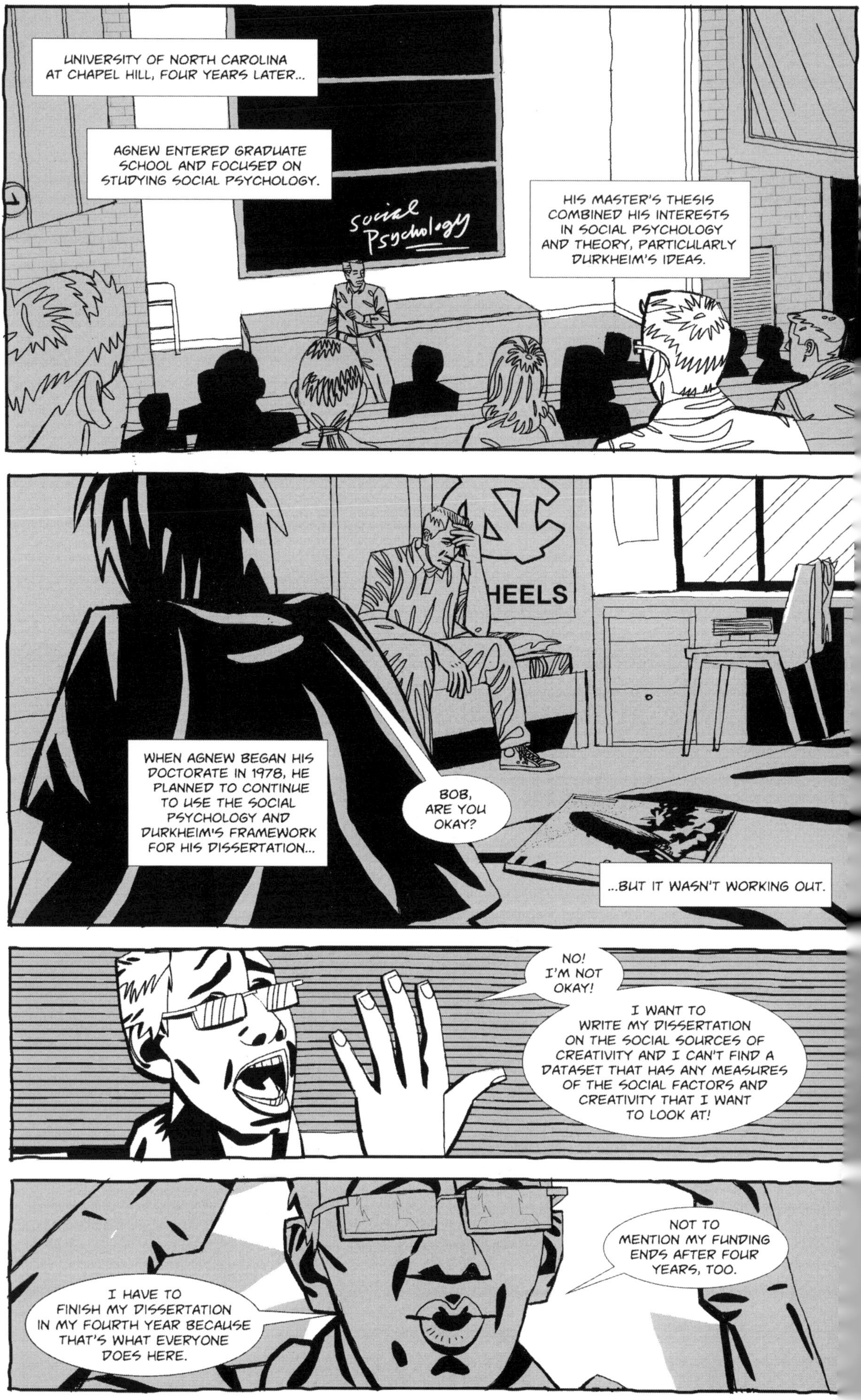

UNIVERSITY OF NORTH CAROLINA AT CHAPEL HILL, FOUR YEARS LATER...
AGNEW ENTERED GRADUATE SCHOOL AND FOCUSED ON STUDYING SOCIAL PSYCHOLOGY.
Social Psychology
HIS MASTER'S THESIS COMBINED HIS INTERESTS IN SOCIAL PSYCHOLOGY AND THEORY, PARTICULARLY DURKHEIM'S IDEAS.
HEELS
WHEN AGNEW BEGAN HIS DOCTORATE IN 1978, HE PLANNED TO CONTINUE TO USE THE SOCIAL PSYCHOLOGY AND DURKHEIM'S FRAMEWORK FOR HIS DISSERTATION...
BOB, ARE YOU OKAY?
...BUT IT WASN'T WORKING OUT.
NO! I'M NOT OKAY!
I WANT TO WRITE MY DISSERTATION ON THE SOCIAL SOURCES OF CREATIVITY AND I CAN'T FIND A DATASET THAT HAS ANY MEASURES OF THE SOCIAL FACTORS AND CREATIVITY THAT I WANT TO LOOK AT!
I HAVE TO FINISH MY DISSERTATION IN MY FOURTH YEAR BECAUSE THAT'S WHAT EVERYONE DOES HERE.
NOT TO MENTION MY FUNDING ENDS AFTER FOUR YEARS, TOO.

DUDE, THAT SOUNDS LIKE A LOT OF PRESSURE. BUT YOU NEED TO CHILL OUT, MAN.

CHECK OUT THE YOUTH IN TRANSITION SURVEY. YOU MIGHT FIND SOMETHING INTERESTING THERE.

THE SURVEY DIDN'T HELP HIM WITH HIS CREATIVITY IDEA, BUT IT HAD MEASURES OF DELINQUENCY, SO AGNEW STARTED READING THE LITERATURE ON THE CAUSES OF DELINQUENCY.

Delinquency and Opportun...

Delinquent B...

SOCIAL SOURCES OF DELINQUENCY

Ruth R. ...nhauser

AUSES of DELINQUE...

WHY DIDN'T I THINK OF THAT?

AGNEW WAS DRAWN TO THE CORE IDEA PROPOSED BY **STRAIN THEORY***—THAT CRIME SOMETIMES RESULTS WHEN PEOPLE CANNOT GET WHAT THEY WANT THROUGH LEGITIMATE MEANS.

THE CLASSIC STRAIN THEORISTS HAVEN'T FOCUSED ON THE STRAINS THAT ARE MOST CONDUCIVE TO CRIME.

SO YOU ARE QUESTIONING ROBERT MERTON'S HYPOTHESIS, MR. AGNEW?

NOT QUESTIONING, SIR, JUST BUILDING ON IT.

WHEN I LOOK AT MY OWN LIFE AND THOSE AROUND ME, NOT BEING ABLE TO ACHIEVE ECONOMIC SUCCESS OR MIDDLE-CLASS STATUS ISN'T A MAJOR STRESSOR CONDUCIVE TO CRIME.

THE MAJOR STRAINS CONDUCIVE TO CRIME SEEM TO BE A BIT MORE IMMEDIATE IN NATURE.

*STRAIN THEORY IS WHAT MANY THEORISTS CALLED MERTON'S THEORY.

"YOU KNOW, LIKE A PEER PUNCHING YOU IN THE FACE..."

"...OR HAVING A SERIOUS ARGUMENT WITH A FAMILY MEMBER."

OR LIKE FINDING A VIABLE AND INTERESTING TOPIC FOR YOUR DISSERTATION?

AHEM...YES, SIR.

THERE IS A PLETHORA OF RESEARCH ON STRESS AND AGGRESSION IN SOCIAL PSYCHOLOGY.

I THINK ANOTHER TYPE OF STRAIN IS THE BLOCKAGE OF PAIN-AVOIDANCE BEHAVIOR.

PEOPLE NOT ONLY TRY TO ACHIEVE CERTAIN GOALS, BUT ALSO TRY TO AVOID PAINFUL OR AVERSIVE SITUATIONS.

BUT LIKE OUR EFFORTS TO ACHIEVE GOALS, EFFORTS TO AVOID PAIN MAY BE BLOCKED TOO.

THIS BLOCKAGE CAN LEAD TO DELINQUENCY BECAUSE IT CREATES ANGER AND FRUSTRATION...

A revised Strain Theory of Delinquency

AFTER COMPLETING HIS DOCTORATE, AGNEW LANDED A CRIMINOLOGY POSITION IN THE SOCIOLOGY DEPARTMENT AT EMORY UNIVERSITY.

IT WAS HERE IN THE 1980S AND EARLY 1990S WHERE HE MODIFIED HIS IDEAS AND ULTIMATELY DEVELOPED HIS *GENERAL STRAIN THEORY (GST)* IN 1992.

OKAY, NOW THAT I'VE PASSED BACK YOUR TESTS, I WANT TO TAKE THIS OPPORTUNITY TO REVISIT GENERAL STRAIN THEORY, SOMETHING THAT WAS COVERED ON THE TEST...

...AND I'M GOING TO FRAME IT IN THE CONTEXT OF STRAINS THAT MAY BE FAMILIAR TO YOU ALL.

failure to achieve posi[t]

AS WE'VE DISCUSSED, THERE ARE THREE TYPES OF STRAINS THAT CAN LEAD TO CRIMINAL BEHAVIOR...

"LET'S SAY YOU STUDIED REALLY HARD FOR THIS TEST AND YOU REALLY REALLY WANTED TO GET A GOOD GRADE."

"OTHER EXAMPLES MIGHT BE NOT MAKING THE SPORTS TEAM OR NOT GETTING A DATE TO A DANCE."

"UNFORTUNATELY, YOU DIDN'T GET THE GRADE YOU WANTED, SO THAT CAN BE VIEWED AS THE FIRST TYPE OF STRAIN: *FAILURE TO ACHIEVE POSITIVELY VALUED GOALS.*"

"THEN AFTER THE TEST, YOU MEET UP WITH YOUR GIRLFRIEND AND SHE BREAKS UP WITH YOU. THIS IS AN EXAMPLE OF THE SECOND TYPE OF STRAIN, *REMOVAL OF POSITIVELY VALUED STIMULI*. OTHER EXAMPLES OF THIS MIGHT INCLUDE THE DEATH OF A LOVED ONE, LOSING A JOB, OR GETTING KICKED OFF AN ATHLETIC TEAM."

BRANDON, I DON'T THINK WE SHOULD SEE EACH OTHER ANYMORE.

"AFTER THIS MEETING, YOU GO BACK TO YOUR DORM AND ENCOUNTER A GUY WHO HAS BEEN BULLYING YOU FOR QUITE SOME TIME. THIS IS THE THIRD SOURCE OF STRAIN: *PRESENTATION OF NEGATIVE OR NOXIOUS STIMULI*. OTHER CAUSES OF THIS TYPE OF STRAIN COULD BE CRIMINAL VICTIMIZATION, EXPERIENCING ABUSE, OR RIDICULE BY PEERS."

WHUMP

BUT MERELY EXPERIENCING THESE STRAINS DOESN'T AUTOMATICALLY MEAN THAT SOMEONE WILL ADAPT BY ENGAGING IN CRIMINAL BEHAVIOR.

TWO OTHER ELEMENTS ARE CRUCIAL IN DETERMINING WHETHER THESE STRAINS WILL LEAD TO CRIME.

"FIRST, THERE ARE THINGS THAT 'CONDITION' A PERSON'S RESPONSE TO STRAIN, AND THESE THINGS WILL AFFECT WHETHER THE PERSON RESPONDS TO THE STRAIN WITH CRIMINAL BEHAVIOR. A PERSON MIGHT DRINK ALCOHOL OR TAKE DRUGS TO MANAGE THE STRESS, RESORT TO ILLEGAL MEANS TO REPLACE WHAT WAS TAKEN AWAY, OR SEEK REVENGE AGAINST THOSE WHO CAUSED THE STRAIN."

"THINGS THAT MAY DIMINISH THE RISK OF CRIMINAL ADAPTATION TO STRAIN INCLUDE INDIVIDUAL *COPING* RESOURCES AND SOCIAL SUPPORT."

C'MON, DUDE. IT'S GOING TO BE OKAY. THERE ARE PLENTY OF OTHER WOMEN OUT THERE WHO WOULD JUMP AT THE CHANCE TO GO ON A DATE WITH YOU!

"THE SECOND ELEMENT RELATES TO EMOTIONS. NEGATIVE EMOTIONS CREATE PRESSURE FOR CORRECTIVE ACTION."

WHO IS THAT GUY WITH HER?!

"THE EMOTION OF *ANGER* IS ESPECIALLY IMPORTANT."

"WHEN STRAIN ELICITS ANGER, CRIME (ESPECIALLY VIOLENT CRIME) IS MORE LIKELY TO OCCUR."

BRANDON!

KRAKK!

PROGRAMS THAT COULD REDUCE CRIME BASED ON GENERAL STRAIN THEORY WOULD INCLUDE TEACHING PROBLEM SOLVING, ANGER MANAGEMENT, AND PROSOCIAL COPING STRATEGIES.

I AM HOPING THAT IF YOU ARE FEELING STRAIN BECAUSE OF YOUR GRADE YOU WILL NOT REACT TO IT WITH ANGER.

HA HA HA

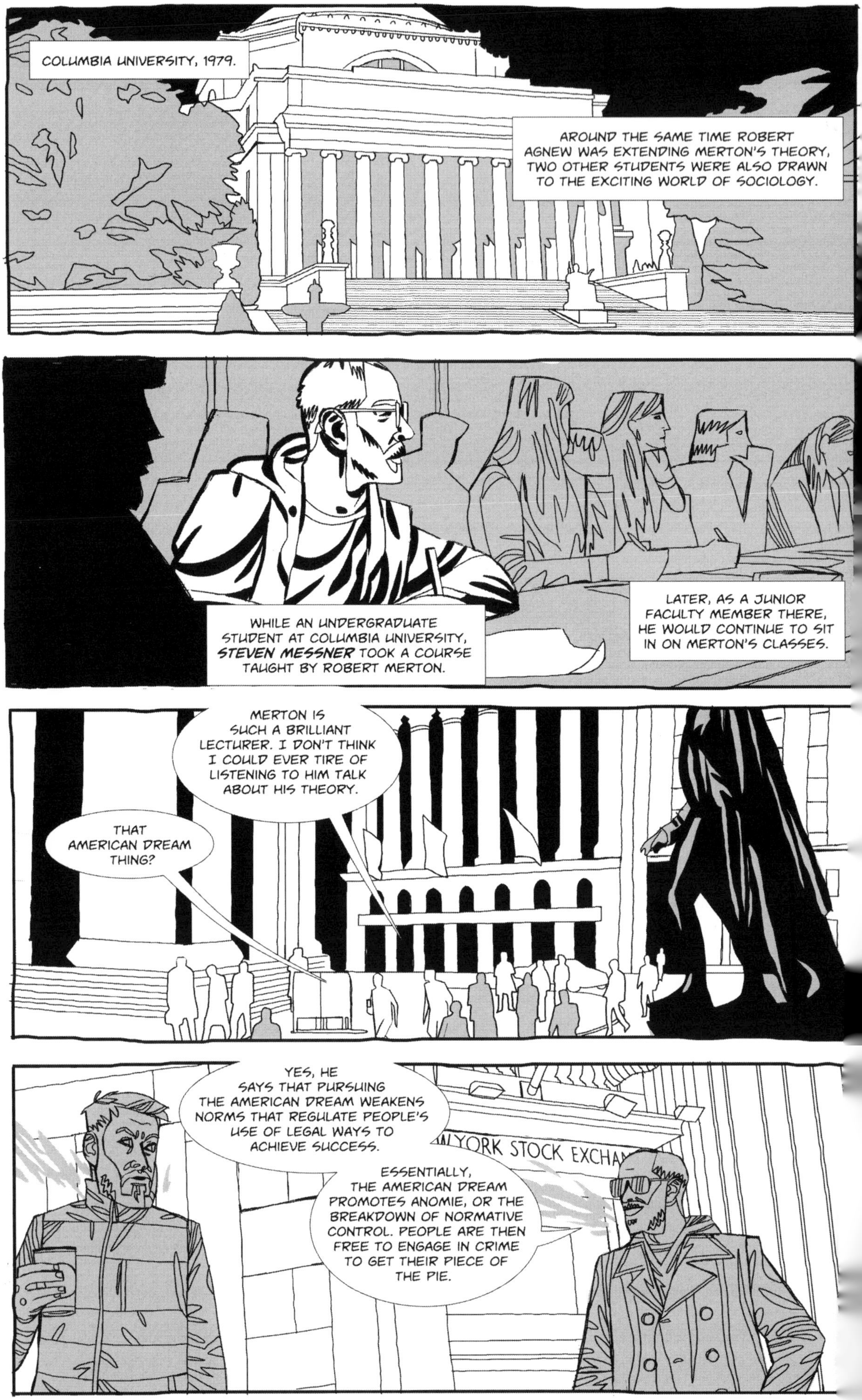
COLUMBIA UNIVERSITY, 1979.
AROUND THE SAME TIME ROBERT AGNEW WAS EXTENDING MERTON'S THEORY, TWO OTHER STUDENTS WERE ALSO DRAWN TO THE EXCITING WORLD OF SOCIOLOGY.
WHILE AN UNDERGRADUATE STUDENT AT COLUMBIA UNIVERSITY, STEVEN MESSNER TOOK A COURSE TAUGHT BY ROBERT MERTON.
LATER, AS A JUNIOR FACULTY MEMBER THERE, HE WOULD CONTINUE TO SIT IN ON MERTON'S CLASSES.
MERTON IS SUCH A BRILLIANT LECTURER. I DON'T THINK I COULD EVER TIRE OF LISTENING TO HIM TALK ABOUT HIS THEORY.
THAT AMERICAN DREAM THING?
YES, HE SAYS THAT PURSUING THE AMERICAN DREAM WEAKENS NORMS THAT REGULATE PEOPLE'S USE OF LEGAL WAYS TO ACHIEVE SUCCESS.
ESSENTIALLY, THE AMERICAN DREAM PROMOTES ANOMIE, OR THE BREAKDOWN OF NORMATIVE CONTROL. PEOPLE ARE THEN FREE TO ENGAGE IN CRIME TO GET THEIR PIECE OF THE PIE.

UNIVERSITY OF OREGON, 1978.

ON THE OPPOSITE COAST, ANOTHER STUDENT WAS EXPLORING THE WRITINGS OF A DIFFERENT SOCIOLOGIST.

RICHARD ROSENFELD WAS INTRODUCED TO THE WRITINGS OF TALCOTT PARSONS* WHEN HE WAS AN UNDERGRADUATE STUDENT.

LATER, AS A GRADUATE STUDENT AT THE UNIVERSITY OF OREGON, ROSENFELD STUDIED WITH BENTON JOHNSON, A STUDENT OF PARSONS AT HARVARD.

*TALCOTT PARSONS WAS ONE OF ROBERT MERTON'S MENTORS.

SO PARSONS TALKS ABOUT SOCIAL INSTITUTIONS AND HOW THEY ARE THE BUILDING BLOCKS OF A SOCIETY.

THEY ARE BROADER AND MORE ABSTRACT THAN THE SOCIAL ORGANIZATIONS THAT COMPRISE THEM.

WHAT'S THE DIFF? AREN'T INSTITUTIONS AND ORGANIZATIONS THE SAME THING?

NOPE. ORGANIZATIONS ARE THINGS LIKE SCHOOLS, CHURCHES, AND SOCIAL SERVICE AGENCIES.

INSTITUTIONS ESTABLISH THE PARAMETERS WITHIN WHICH THE ORGANIZATIONS OPERATE.

INSTITUTIONS ARE THINGS LIKE FAMILY, EDUCATION, RELIGION, OR GOVERNMENT.

AMERICAN SOCIETY OF CRIMINOLOGY MEETING.

IN THE MID-1980S, MESSNER WAS AT THE STATE UNIVERSITY OF NEW YORK AT ALBANY AND ROSENFELD WAS AT SKIDMORE COLLEGE IN SARASOTA SPRINGS.

HEY STEVE, I WANT TO INTRODUCE YOU TO RICK. RICK AND I WERE ON A PANEL LAST YEAR.

PROFESSIONAL CONFERENCES ALLOWED THEM AND OTHER FACULTY AND SCHOLARS TO GATHER AND SHARE THEIR RESEARCH.

I THINK MERTON'S THEORY IS BRILLIANT, AND I APPRECIATE HOW IT IDENTIFIES THE CENTRAL ROLE THE AMERICAN DREAM PLAYS IN GENERATING CRIMINAL BEHAVIOR...

...THE AMERICAN DREAM BEING A COMMITMENT TO THE GOAL OF MATERIAL SUCCESS THAT IS PURSUED BY EVERYONE IN SOCIETY UNDER THE CONDITIONS OF OPEN, INDIVIDUAL COMPETITION.

BUT DON'T YOU THINK HIS INSTITUTIONAL ANALYSIS IS LACKING?

DEFINITELY! HIS THEORY FOCUSED ON AMERICA'S ECONOMIC INSTITUTION, BUT DIDN'T DISCUSS THE SOCIAL ARRANGEMENTS OF OTHER INSTITUTIONS IN THE UNITED STATES.

THESE CONVERSATIONS ULTIMATELY LED TO THEIR DEVELOPMENT OF *INSTITUTIONAL-ANOMIE THEORY*. THIS THEORY WAS OUTLINED IN THEIR BOOK *CRIME AND THE AMERICAN DREAM* (1994).

IN THIS THEORY, THEY PROPOSED THAT THE REASON THE UNITED STATES HAD SUCH A HIGH CRIME RATE WAS DUE TO AN INSTITUTIONAL BALANCE OF POWER TILTED TOWARD THE ECONOMY.

A SOCIETY CONSISTS OF STRUCTURAL ARRANGEMENTS OF SOCIAL INSTITUTIONS, INCLUDING THE FAMILY, EDUCATION, RELIGION, GOVERNMENT, AND ECONOMY.

IN THE UNITED STATES, THE ECONOMIC INSTITUTION DOMINATES OTHER SOCIAL INSTITUTIONS.

NONECONOMIC INSTITUTIONS IN THE UNITED STATES ARE ARRANGED TO BE SUBSERVIENT TO THE ECONOMY.

FOR EXAMPLE, EDUCATION IS SEEN AS A MEANS TO A HIGHER PAYING JOB.

STUDENTS WHO MAJOR IN DISCIPLINES THAT CANNOT TYPICALLY BE LINKED TO HIGH-PAYING, SECURE EMPLOYMENT ARE OFTEN RIDICULED AS WASTING THEIR TIME.

SO WHAT'S YOUR MAJOR?

ENGLISH.

WHAT KIND OF JOB CAN YOU GET WITH THAT?

PURSUIT OF EMPLOYMENT OFTEN UPENDS FAMILY VALUES AND STABILITY.

EVERYONE, I HAVE AN ANNOUNCEMENT-- I GOT THE PROMOTION.

WE'RE MOVING TO ST. LOUIS IN 3 MONTHS.

IF THEY WERE STRONGER, THESE NONECONOMIC INSTITUTIONS COULD DEMAND A LEVEL OF INVOLVEMENT THAT CONSTRAINED BEHAVIOR.

HOWEVER, BECAUSE OF THEIR SUBSERVIENCE TO THE ECONOMY, THEY LOSE THEIR ABILITY TO SOCIALIZE AND CONTROL THE CITIZENRY.

IN THE UNITED STATES, THE HIGH RATE OF SERIOUS CRIME IS CAUSED BY A DISTINCT, MUTUALLY REINFORCING CULTURE AND INSTITUTIONAL STRUCTURE.

THE AMERICAN DREAM IS A POWERFUL CULTURAL FORCE THAT GENERATES ANOMIE BY MOTIVATING THE PURSUIT OF ECONOMIC SUCCESS THROUGH ANY MEANS POSSIBLE.

OFTENTIMES, THIS MAY INVOLVE CRIMINAL BEHAVIOR.

ONE WAY TO COMBAT THIS IS *DECOMMODIFICATION* OF LABOR. THAT IS, IMPLEMENT POLICIES THAT INSULATE PERSONAL WELL-BEING FROM PURE MARKET FORCES (E.G., FAMILY SUPPORT, SOCIAL SECURITY, UNEMPLOYMENT INSURANCE).

HIGHLY DECOMMODIFIED POLICIES, IN THE FORM OF BROAD AND GENEROUS SOCIAL WELFARE AND INSURANCE PROGRAMS, COULD LOWER CRIME RATES BY BALANCING THE POWER OF THE SOCIAL INSTITUTIONS.

WHATCHA WRITING?

OH, IT'S JUST A POEM I'M WRITING FOR A CLASS.

THAT'S JUST WONDERFUL! I LOVE YOUR POETRY!

THIS ISSUE BEGAN WITH A DISCUSSION OF THE DEVELOPMENT OF ROBERT MERTON'S ANOMIE THEORY. MERTON BORROWED THE TERM ANOMIE FROM EMILE DURKHEIM, A FRENCH SOCIOLOGIST, WHO PROPOSED ANOMIE DEVELOPED WHEN INSTITUTIONALIZED NORMS LOST THEIR ABILITY TO REGULATE HUMAN NEEDS AND BEHAVIORS. AS SOCIETY MODERNIZED, GREAT EMPHASIS WAS PLACED ON "ACHIEVING INDUSTRIAL PROSPERITY" WITHOUT RESTRAINING PEOPLE'S APPETITE FOR SUCCESS. MERTON USED THIS CONCEPT TO DEVELOP A SOCIOLOGICAL EXPLANATION FOR CRIME AT A TIME WHEN THEORIZING ABOUT CRIME FOCUSED ON INDIVIDUAL FACTORS. HE PROPOSED THAT SOCIETY CONSISTED OF A CULTURAL STRUCTURE AND A SOCIAL STRUCTURE THAT WERE NOT INTEGRATED. THE CULTURAL STRUCTURE CONSISTS OF CULTURALLY DEFINED GOALS (THE AMERICAN DREAM) AND INSTITUTIONAL NORMS (ACCEPTABLE MODES OF ACHIEVING THESE GOALS). THE SOCIAL STRUCTURE RELATES TO CLASS STRATIFICATION, WHICH IMPACTS PEOPLE'S ACCESS TO THE MEANS TO REACH THESE GOALS. WHEN PEOPLE DO NOT HAVE THE INSTITUTIONAL MEANS TO REACH CULTURALLY PRESCRIBED GOALS, IT CAUSES STRAIN ON INSTITUTIONAL NORMS. THE NORMS THEN LOSE THEIR LEGITIMACY AND REGULATORY POWER, THUS FREEING PEOPLE TO PURSUE GOALS IN ANY WAY THEY SEE FIT. IN ADDITION, MERTON PROPOSED THERE WERE INDIVIDUAL ADAPTATIONS TO THIS SITUATION. WHEN FACED WITH A GAP BETWEEN GOALS AND THE MEANS TO ACHIEVE THOSE GOALS, AN INDIVIDUAL WILL FEEL STRAIN. ADAPTATIONS TO STRAIN INCLUDE CONFORMITY, INNOVATION, RITUALISM, RETREATISM, AND REBELLION.

ROBERT AGNEW APPRECIATED MERTON'S EXPLANATION OF CRIME, BUT HE BELIEVED IT WAS TOO NARROW. INSTEAD OF ONE SOURCE OF STRAIN (ECONOMIC), AGNEW PROPOSED THERE ARE OTHER MORE IMMEDIATE CAUSES OF STRAIN THAT MAY CAUSE INDIVIDUALS TO COMMIT CRIME. IN GENERAL STRAIN THEORY, HE PROPOSED THREE SOURCES OF STRAIN: (1) FAILURE TO ACHIEVE POSITIVELY VALUED GOALS, (2) REMOVAL OF POSITIVELY VALUED STIMULI, AND (3) PRESENTATION OF NEGATIVE STIMULI. WHETHER A PERSON RESPONDS TO STRAIN WITH CRIMINAL BEHAVIOR DEPENDS ON HIS OR HER COPING MECHANISMS AND WHETHER THE STRAIN CAUSES NEGATIVE AFFECTIVE STATES, ESPECIALLY ANGER.

STEVEN MESSNER AND RICHARD ROSENFELD ALSO EXTENDED MERTON'S ANOMIE THEORY BY EXPANDING THE INSTITUTIONAL ANALYSIS OF THE THEORY. THEY PROPOSED THAT THE REASON THE UNITED STATES HAD SUCH A HIGH CRIME RATE WAS DUE TO AN INSTITUTIONAL BALANCE OF POWER TILTED TOWARD THE ECONOMY. BECAUSE THE ECONOMIC INSTITUTION DOMINATES OTHER SOCIAL INSTITUTIONS IN THE UNITED STATES, NONECONOMIC INSTITUTIONS BECOME SUBSERVIENT TO THE ECONOMY AND LOSE THEIR ABILITY TO SOCIALIZE AND CONTROL THE CITIZENRY.

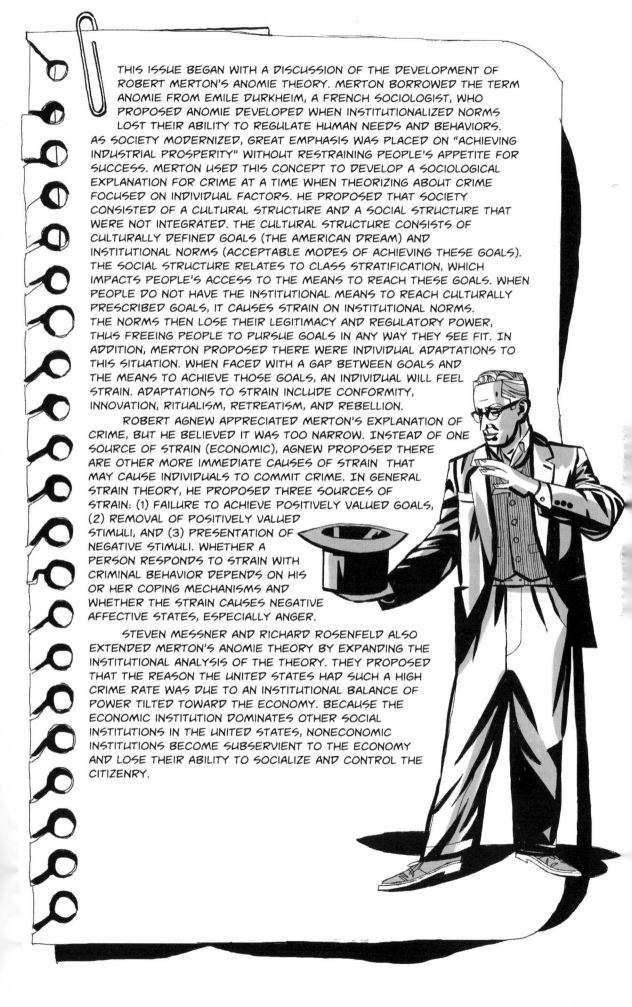

Key Terms

Robert King Merton
Sociology
Emile Durkheim
Anomie
Great Depression
Cultural Structure
Social Structure
American Dream
Institutional Norms
Strain
Modes of Adaptation
Conformity
Innovation
Ritualism
Retreatism
Rebellion
Robert Agnew
Strain Theory
General Strain Theory (GST)
Failure to Achieve Positively Valued Goals
Removal of Positively Valued Stimuli
Presentation of Negative or Noxious Stimuli
Coping
Anger
Steven Messner
Richard Rosenfeld
Talcott Parsons
Social Institutions
Institutional-Anomie Theory
Decommodification

Discussion Questions

Describe what the American Dream is. Do you believe that Merton's theory explains crime adequately, both at the aggregate and at the individual level? Explain your answer.

Provide examples of the five adaptations to strain that you see in your own life.

Provide examples of the three sources of strain proposed by general strain theory (not presented in this text). Does this theory adequately explain criminal behavior? Explain.

How could we reduce crime by implementing policies, practices, or programs grounded in institutional-anomie theory?

Suggested Readings

Agnew, R. (1985). A revised strain theory of delinquency. *Social Forces, 64,* 151–167.

Agnew, R. (1992). Foundation for a general strain theory of crime and delinquency. *Criminology, 30,* 47–87.

Agnew, R. (2005). *Pressured into crime.* New York: Oxford University Press.

Cullen, F. T., Agnew, R., & Wilcox, P. (2014). *Criminological theory: Past to present* (5th ed.). New York: Oxford University Press.

Lilly, J. R., Cullen, F. T., & Ball, R. (2015). *Criminological theory: Context and consequences* (6th ed.). Los Angeles: Sage Publications.

Merton, R. (1938). Social structure and anomie. *American Sociological Review, 3,* 672–682.

Messner, S., & Rosenfeld, R. (2013). *Crime and the American Dream* (5th ed.). Belmont, CA: Wadsworth Publishing.